USDA

United States
Department of
Agriculture

Forest Service

Pacific Northwest
Research Station

Research Paper
PNW-RP-581
June 2009

Public Acceptance of Disturbance-Based Forest Management: A Study of the Blue River Landscape Strategy in the Central Cascades Adaptive Management Area

Bruce Shindler and Angela L. Mallon

Authors

Bruce Shindler is a professor and **Angela L. Mallon** is a faculty research assistant, Department of Forest Ecosystems and Society, Oregon State University, Corvallis, OR 97331. Project research was conducted under Agreement 05-CR-11061801-013 between Oregon State University and the U.S. Department of Agriculture, Forest Service, Willamette National Forest, with the cooperation of the Bureau of Land Management, Eugene (OR) District.

Abstract

Shindler, Bruce; Mallon, Angela L. 2009. Public acceptance of disturbance-based forest management: a study of the Blue River Landscape Strategy in the Central Cascades Adaptive Management Area. Res. Pap. PNW-RP-581. Portland, OR: U.S. Department of Agriculture, Forest Service, Pacific Northwest Research Station. 42 p.

This report examines public perspectives on disturbance-based management conducted in the central Cascade Range in Oregon as part of the Blue River Landscape Strategy. A mail survey to local residents was used to describe the public's understanding of this form of management, identify perceived associated risks and potential barriers to implementation, and the overall level of support for disturbance-based practices. Findings suggest the public generally supports the disturbance-based concept, particularly ecological benefits, but many individuals are still uncertain about details and are withholding judgment until they see the outcomes of implementation. Support is highly correlated with citizens' past interaction with local managers. Major concerns involve the amount of timber harvesting necessary to achieve objectives and the possibility that changing national politics may influence the consistency of agency policies toward disturbance-based management.

Keywords: Disturbance-based management, historical range of variability, social acceptability, citizen-agency interactions.

Summary

Introduction and Study Objectives

This report provides a detailed summary of research conducted on public acceptability of disturbance-based forest management in the Central Cascades Adaptive Management Area (CCAMA). Growing emphasis on ecosystem and landscape-level forest management across North America has spurred an examination of alternative management strategies that focus on emulating dynamic natural disturbance processes, particularly those associated with forest fire regimes. This topic is the cornerstone of research in the Blue River Landscape Study (BRLS) taking place in the CCAMA, located in the McKenzie River watershed of western Oregon. Public acceptability plays a critical role in the success of ecosystem management practices. Although there is a substantial body of research on citizen support for the concept of ecosystem management, less is known about public perceptions and opinions about specific management practices. Within this context, this study examines the perceptions of disturbance-based management held by members of the attentive public in McKenzie River watershed communities and the cities of Eugene and Springfield. The attentive public is considered to be those individuals who pay attention to local forest issues and are often the first ones to respond to new plans and practices. Analysis is based upon responses to a mail survey conducted in 2005–06. Overall, 230 of 312 questionnaires were completed for a 74-percent response rate.

The purposes of research with this highly relevant population of citizens are threefold: (1) to examine citizens' understanding of and support for disturbance-based management and their perceptions of risk and uncertainty associated with it, (2) to gather information that will help federal agencies communicate and engage with the public about this topic while building literacy among citizens about the disturbance-based approach, and (3) to satisfy terms of a 2003 settlement agreement between the Bureau of Land Management and American Forest Resources Council[1] that requires assessment of public acceptance of disturbance-based management.

---

[1] U.S. Department of Agriculture; U.S. Department of the Interior [USDA and USDI]. 2003. Departments of Agriculture and Interior proposed settlement agreement with the American Forest Resource Council. http://www.blm.gov/or/plans/wopr/settlement.php. (28 April 2009).

The specific objectives of this study focused on gathering information about the following:

- Citizen knowledge of general forest management practices and ecosystem processes.
- Interactions with and trust in forest management agencies in the area.
- Public perceptions of risk associated with disturbance-based management.
- Knowledge of key concepts and practices associated with disturbance-based management.
- Potential barriers to disturbance-based management.
- The overall level of support for this approach, including citizen-agency interactions and public trust in forest agencies to implement management practices.

Key Findings

Overall, findings from this study indicate that McKenzie watershed citizens are cautiously supportive of disturbance-based management, with a number of important qualifications. These include:

- More than half of study participants say they support disturbance-based management. However, a substantial segment (27 percent) is uncertain about this approach, indicating that citizens may not have a full understanding of disturbance-based management on which to base their judgments, or may be waiting to see the outcomes of implementation.
- Timber harvest associated with disturbance-based management is a primary concern, particularly the potential for excessive thinning, increased road building, and harvest in old-growth stands.
- Most respondents (85 percent) believe forest reserves (areas with no commercial timber harvest) are necessary for plant and animal conservation in the McKenzie watershed.
- Citizens displayed awareness and concern that changing national politics can influence the consistency of agency policies toward disturbance-based management. For example, although they may trust their local ranger district to implement projects, they have less confidence that the federal government will let local personnel make good on these decisions.
- Among the areas of least concern for study participants is the idea that a disturbance-based approach needs to pay for itself. These findings suggest that the citizens sampled are more interested in ecological benefits than in economic return from these practices.

- Citizens' past interactions with agency employees is the variable most highly correlated with support for disturbance-based management—the more favorable citizens' opinions about past interactions are, the greater their support for disturbance-based management.

Other key findings include:

- In all areas of the survey, there were few significant differences between the opinions of Eugene-Springfield residents and their counterparts in upriver communities.
- McKenzie citizens possess high levels of formal education, and over 90 percent pay a moderate to a great deal of attention to national forest issues.
- Perceptions of overall forest health in the McKenzie watershed are mixed. Over one-quarter of respondents view forests as unhealthy, and 61 percent see them as healthy.
- A substantial proportion of the study population places priority on environmental objectives over economic ones in forest management.
- Although the attentive public in the McKenzie watershed has a high level of knowledge with respect to basic ecosystem management, they have a lower level of understanding about specific disturbance-based management techniques. Terminology associated with the latter approach is not intuitive for most citizens.
- Citizens generally have high levels of confidence in scientists and scientific information, and approve of scientific experimentation on federal forest lands.
- Inability to identify with central focus points of disturbance-based management may be problematic in message communication. Currently, less than a quarter of the respondents know about the CCAMA or the BRLS.
- Face-to-face interactive forms of communication between agencies and citizens are rated as most useful for communicating about new management approaches. Citizens also rate newspapers and newsletters as useful for general dissemination of information.
- Public confidence in agencies and the information they provide appears to be relatively low, although McKenzie watershed citizens tend to trust local agency personnel more than those at the federal or regional levels. Many respondents indicated they trust local agency personnel to make management decisions, but are concerned that politics at the national level prevent them from implementing these decisions.

Based on these findings, several conclusions can be made. First, citizens in McKenzie communities can make important contributions to planning new management strategies. For example, these individuals could be engaged in meaningful ways from the very beginning in decisionmaking processes. Doing so will not only improve the quality of information used to make decisions, but can also serve to build support and acceptance for new approaches as these individuals help carry the message to the broader community.

Second, clarification of objectives and rationale behind disturbance-based management approaches will better serve the public. Currently, terminology and techniques associated with this approach are not well understood among local citizens. To increase relevancy, the disturbance-based concept will need to be presented in a context that has meaning for citizens, such as addressing forest health or species conservation problems, particularly in places familiar to residents.

Third, agencies can capitalize on the existing high level of public knowledge about forests and ecosystem processes to cultivate further understanding of disturbance-emulating techniques. Interactive outreach settings—including conversations with agency personnel and scientists, field trips, and small workshops—can be successful in increasing knowledge of projects, and are also effective at building relationships between agencies and citizens.

Fourth, agencies can help citizens become more comfortable with this concept by addressing issues of risk and uncertainty associated with a disturbance-based management approach. These issues are often primary factors in the public's willingness to accept forest management practices, particularly those that are new and largely untested. Citizen understanding of the potential for risk provides a context in which managers and scientists can discuss how mistakes or unintended consequences of disturbance-based management can be dealt with.

Finally, an emphasis on improving citizen-agency interactions, not just on a project basis but as a central long-term goal, is essential. Citizens respect and respond to agency personnel they view as trustworthy and credible. They make their judgments based on agency actions and followthrough, particularly those intended to include public perspectives. For this reason, positive interactions are most effectively initiated and maintained at the local community level. Improving citizen-agency interactions will involve treating trust-building as a central, long-term goal of an organized public outreach program.

Contents

Introduction

In recent decades, federal forest management in the Pacific Northwest has shifted from a focus on sustained-yield timber harvest through dispersed and aggregated patch clearcutting to a system of management based on static land allocations laid out by the Northwest Forest Plan. However, growing emphasis on ecosystem and landscape management has spurred interest in alternative management strategies that focus on dynamic natural processes (Cissel et al. 1999, Parsons et al. 1998). One such method is the use of historical disturbance as a guide for ecosystem management, which involves applying information about past natural disturbances to inform practices such as timber harvest, prescribed burning, or wildfire suppression (Perera and Buse 2004). It is largely a coarse-filter approach with a primary objective of conserving native species.

As scientists and managers work to unravel the ecological and economic implications of disturbance-based management, they must also consider public acceptance for such an approach. Numerous studies have demonstrated the importance of understanding the role of citizen values and attitudes in ecosystem management (Clawson 1975, Firey 1960, Grumbine 1994, Shindler et al. 2002c). Decisions based solely on biological science can lead to policy failures; for this reason, ecological research must be supplemented with investigations into relevant social perspectives of forest management processes and practices (Endter-Wada et al. 1998). However, although the body of knowledge is large with respect to public perceptions of ecosystem management as a concept, much less is known about citizen attitudes toward and support for methods for achieving specific objectives, particularly options for relatively new ideas like disturbance-based management (Shindler 2000).

This report summarizes research on stakeholder attitudes toward and support for the use of historical disturbance as a guide for future forest management in the Blue River Landscape Study (BRLS). The BRLS is one of several projects underway in the Central Cascades Adaptive Management Area (CCAMA), an area designated for joint experimentation by the Willamette National Forest and the Bureau of Land Management Eugene District in conjunction with the research community. Our research encompassed both Bureau of Land Management (BLM) and Forest Service personnel in the CCAMA as well as members of the attentive public in the McKenzie River watershed and the cities of Eugene and Springfield. In this study, attentive public is defined as citizens who have demonstrated past interest in local forest issues through participation in field trips, attendance at planning meetings, submission of input during public comment periods, or putting their name on a mailing list for information. The attentive public is being targeted with the expectation that knowledge of and interest in ecosystem management will be higher in this cohort, an assumption supported by the research of Wright (2000) and Williams (2001). These individuals are often the first to be affected by new management programs on public lands and thus are the first to respond to these initiatives (Shindler 2003). They represent an important stakeholder group—as well as an important barometer of public opinion—with which forest agencies will need to interact for program implementation over the long term.

Exploratory in nature, the public component of this study focused on gathering information about (1) citizen knowledge of general forest management practices and ecosystem processes, (2) interaction with and trust in forest management agencies in the area, (3) perceptions of risk associated with disturbance-based management, (4) knowledge of key concepts and practices associated with disturbance-based management, (5) potential barriers to disturbance-based management, and (6) the overall level of support for this approach.

This research has three primary purposes. The first is to examine the nature of citizens' attitudes and perceptions of disturbance-based management so that resource professionals in the CCAMA may weigh the feasibility of this management approach and discern how to better communicate with the public about it. In this respect, areas of particular interest are the level of understanding about disturbance-based management possessed by members of the attentive public, their support for this approach, and their perceptions of the associated risks or uncertainties.

The second purpose is to provide information that will enable agency personnel to more fully communicate and engage with the public in developing ecosystem management strategies while at the same time increasing citizen literacy about these techniques. Third, this research will satisfy conditions laid out in an August 2003 settlement agreement between the American Forest Resources Council and the BLM stemming from a lawsuit concerning the legal status of reserves on some BLM lands. As part of this agreement, the CCAMA is charged with several tasks, including assessing public understanding and the acceptability of disturbance-based management. This report addresses this task.

Research Setting

The CCAMA is located in the McKenzie River watershed, an area that extends from the crest of the Cascade Mountain Range to the Willamette River in west-central Oregon. Within this watershed are located several small communities (e.g., McKenzie Bridge, Leaburg, and Vida) as well as many popular outdoor recreation sites along the McKenzie River and on upland forests. The nearest metropolitan area is Eugene/Springfield with a combined population of 206,000 people, located at the confluence of the Willamette and McKenzie Rivers (U.S. Census Bureau 2007). The upriver population of the watershed generally comprises retirees, people employed in either recreation- or extraction-based natural resource economies, and residents who commute to jobs in the Eugene/Springfield area (Shindler et al. 1996).

Area residents use Willamette National Forest lands and BLM lands frequently, and many of them claim to pay a moderate or great deal of attention to forest management issues (Shindler et al. 1996). Furthermore, several studies of citizen perspectives in the area have shown residents place great value on participation in forest management decisionmaking and planning processes (Shindler et al. 1996, Williams 2001, Wright 2000).

Management Context

Research in ecosystem management has a long history in the McKenzie River watershed. In 1948, the H.J. Andrews Experimental Forest was established in the Lookout Creek drainage, one of the tributaries to the McKenzie River. Research in forest and stream ecosystem dynamics has been underway there since the 1950s, and pioneering research on the structure and function of old-growth forest ecosystems began in the 1970s (Andrews Experimental Forest LTER 2002, FEMAT 1993). In 1991, the Cascade Center for Ecosystem Management was established to facilitate integration of historical research at the H.J. Andrews with new research projects (CCEM 2001). One of these is the BRLS, which is designed to develop and evaluate disturbance-based management objectives for the 57,000-acre Blue River Watershed (Rapp 2003). The stated purpose of the BRLS is to use historical disturbance regimes as a model for management activities intended to achieve the objectives of the Northwest Forest Plan: late-successional habitat, aquatic ecosystems, and sustainable timber production (CCEM 2001).

The BRLS area and the H.J. Andrews Experimental Forest are both contained within the boundaries of the CCAMA, one of 10 adaptive management areas (AMAs) established by the 1994 Northwest Forest Plan. The total area of the CCAMA is 158,000 acres, the majority of which is located in the McKenzie River watershed, although a small section extends into the South Santiam River watershed (Shindler et al. 1996). Experiments and projects at the CCAMA have benefited from collaborative efforts and good relationships between scientists and managers at the AMA, the Andrews Forest, and the nearby McKenzie River Ranger District.

Managers at the CCAMA, like those at most AMAs, confront many challenges in implementing adaptive management practices. These include coordination and cooperation across jurisdictional boundaries (Stankey and Shindler 1997), working within the context of a changing political climate (Shindler et al. 1999), and balancing the demands of managing adaptively on time and resources that must also be devoted to the day-to-day business (Stankey and Shindler 1997). Furthermore, managers in the CCAMA face questions about how to appropriately involve and communicate with the public in planning activities as well as how to determine the public's expectations for successful outcomes (Shindler and Neburka 1995). Indeed, in a study of public judgments toward CCAMA managers conducted early in the AMA program, Shindler et al. (1996) found that just one-third of the participants believed the Forest Service and BLM were open to public input and use it in making decisions. This research, in addition to that conducted by Shindler, Williams, and Wright in 2002 with the attentive public, form the foundation for inquiries into the nature of interactions between agency personnel and McKenzie watershed citizens (Shindler et al. 2002a).

With regard to the specific objectives of the BRLS, managers must address questions such as how natural variability is defined and past conditions are described, both spatially and temporally, as well as the challenges presented by unexpected disturbance events occurring in the present (Landres et al. 1999). Public support for such research has been demonstrated in a previous CCAMA study (Shindler et al. 1996), where two-thirds of the participants agreed with scientific experimentation in forest ecosystems. However, resource professionals will need to navigate the transition between the theoretical phases of project planning and on-the-ground implementation.

Objectives

In spite of substantial inquiry into citizen attitudes toward forest ecosystem management in general, research regarding perceptions and opinions of historical disturbance-based management in the United States is extremely limited. Thus, small case studies of places where these practices are underway are particularly useful. One study site includes communities in the McKenzie River watershed. The study objectives were to:

1. Assess stakeholder understanding of natural disturbance processes and disturbance-based management techniques.
2. Examine public acceptance for disturbance-based management and the forest agencies who will implement these practices.
3. Assess stakeholder concerns about the risk and uncertainty in this approach.
4. Explore potential barriers to future implementation of disturbance-based management.

Methods

This assessment of stakeholder attitudes toward disturbance-based management employed a combination of qualitative and quantitative methods, which included focus group interviews during visits to selected field sites, individual interviews, and a mail questionnaire. Interviews and focus groups were primarily used in the initial phases of the research to inform the design of the mail questionnaire. They were used in a lesser degree to add insight to quantitative data analysis. The combination of both quantitative and qualitative methods enabled a broad inquiry into factors that influence public attitudes, which is not normally achieved by applying either method alone (Babbie 2001).

However, this report focuses directly on the quantitative survey data.

Interviews and Focus Groups

Prior to the focus group field trips, semistructured interviews were conducted with two researchers instrumental in initiating the BRLS and in constructing research objectives for the project. These interviews helped to identify themes and questions that could be covered in field trip discussions.

Focus groups are frequently used in the first stages of research on new topics, with the purpose of identifying themes of interest and concern among stakeholder groups. Because disturbance-based management is a relatively new concept, focus groups were conducted in conjunction with two field trips to sites in the BRLS area. One trip involved agency managers and researchers; the other included both agency personnel and citizens. These field visits achieved three purposes: to familiarize participants with the concept of disturbance-based management, to view and discuss examples of implementation of the concept, and to lend context to discussions about the BRLS approach.

Field trips took place on two days during the spring of 2005. The first field trip included 19 personnel (15 managers, 4 researchers) from the Willamette National Forest, Eugene District BLM, and H.J. Andrews Experimental Forest. Participants visited three sites that had harvesting treatments designed to emulate various fire regimes. Discussion during the agency tour was primarily focused on the challenges of implementing disturbance-based management in the BRLS; the reasons for using this approach; risk and uncertainty surrounding it; and support for disturbance-based management, both internal to the agencies and externally among the public. The information obtained from this trip was used to identify issues for discussion on the public field tour and also to further inform questionnaire design for the mail survey. Information from the agency site visits is not otherwise a topic of this report.

The second field trip included nine members of the attentive public from McKenzie River communities, with eight agency personnel along to describe treatments of each site. Citizen participants were selected based on their status as leaders within their communities or as individuals interested in forest issues in the McKenzie River watershed. These individuals included business leaders, private landowners, and members of the McKenzie Watershed Council. Forest Service personnel who were familiar with communities in the McKenzie helped to identify and recruit participants for the tour. Participants on this trip visited two sites demonstrating the disturbance-based management approach. To initiate discussion, agency personnel described the specific treatments implemented at each site. Group discussion then focused on the appropriateness of disturbance-based management, concerns and uncertainty surrounding this approach, reactions to treatments, political realities of a long-term strategy, and confidence in agencies to implement this approach. Group interaction was generally informal with all participants joining in by expressing questions, answers, and opinions. This discussion also revealed the citizens' level of understanding of the concept of disturbance-based management and the terms used to describe it.

Mail Survey

An 8-page mail questionnaire was developed based on the themes identified during the focus group field trips, interviews, and a review of research literature. Survey questions addressed respondents' knowledge of forest management in general and disturbance processes in particular, opinions about forest management practices, support for disturbance-based management, and interactions with federal agencies for implementation of this approach. Draft surveys were reviewed by research collaborators at Oregon State University.

The survey was distributed to a sample of 312 individuals from the attentive public. This sample was drawn from three primary sources: an existing Forest Service list of individuals who requested information about management activities or attended public meetings or field trips; the newsletter mailing list for the McKenzie Watershed Council; and a mailing list developed by Oregon State University researchers studying public perceptions of the CCAMA. Only residents of the McKenzie Watershed and Eugene-Springfield were included in the sample.

Questionnaires were mailed with a hand-signed cover letter and self-addressed, stamped return envelope according to a modified "total design method" (Dillman 1978). Overall, 230 surveys were completed and returned resulting in a response rate of 74 percent. Market research analysis indicates this level of response to be sufficiently high to make inferences to the larger study population of the attentive public in the McKenzie River watershed (Lehman 1989).

Findings

Study findings are presented in written, graphical, and tabular format in the following sections: (1) participant profile, public awareness of forest issues, and knowledge of ecosystem processes; (2) opinions about forest management practices, citizen-agency interactions, and use of information sources; and (3) support for disturbance-based management. In some cases, categories have been collapsed for presentation purposes (i.e., "agree" and "strongly agree" combined into a single category, "agree"). Table footnotes indicate when responses between upriver and Eugene-Springfield participant groups were significantly different. All table values are in percentages unless otherwise indicated.

Participant Profile, Public Awareness, and Knowledge

The demographic characteristics shown in table 1 provide a context for understanding responses of survey participants. This information will be used to identify trends associated with different population segments. Findings are arranged so that differences between responses from upriver communities (rural) and the more urban area of Eugene-Springfield (E/S) can be identified.

Table 1—Respondent characteristics

	Overall	Eugene/Springfield	Upriver
Total sample size	230	133	97
Mean years of residence in Lane County	32	33	32
Gender:			
Male (percent)	74	7	70
Female (percent)	27	24	30
Mean age	60	59	61
Education:[a]			
Some high school (percent)	1	0	2
High school (percent)	5	4	7
Some college (percent)	23	17	33
Bachelor's degree (percent)	25	29	20
Some graduate school (percent)	15	16	14
Graduate degree (percent)	30	35	25

[a] Eugene-Springfield respondents possessed significantly higher levels of education.

Overall, the sample is dominated by males, although a slightly greater proportion of rural females than urban females responded. This result is consistent with results from other forest management surveys. The mean age (60 years) is slightly greater than the mean age of respondents from past similar studies (Shindler et al. 2002b, Williams 2001), perhaps reflecting an important characteristic of the attentive public–possession of free time to pay attention to natural resource issues.

Two findings are particularly noteworthy. One is the average length of residency in the McKenzie River watershed (32 years), which is related in part to the average age of survey respondents. Recent research suggests long-term residency corresponds to a high level of knowledge of and attention to forest issues (Shindler and Toman 2002). Also of interest is the high level of education indicated by survey respondents—70 percent of the total have earned a bachelor's degree or higher. Eugene-Springfield respondents have significantly higher levels of education than upriver residents.

Public awareness—

To test the notion that our sample represented the "attentive public," participants were first asked to indicate how much attention they pay to national forest issues or problems. Previous studies have linked self-rated awareness of forest-related issues to knowledge about forest management practices (Shindler and Toman 2002, Williams 2001). In this case, 94 percent of participants indicated they pay a moderate to a great deal of attention to national forest issues (fig. 1).

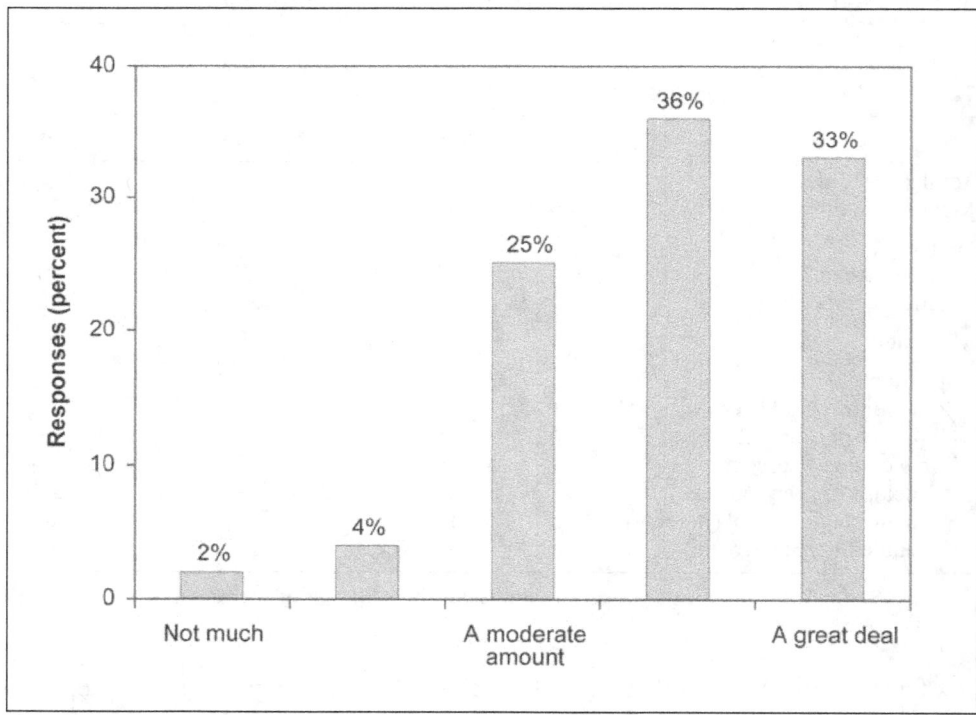

Figure 1—How much attention do you pay to national forest issues or problems?

Policy orientation—

Respondents were next asked to rank their forest policy orientation on a seven-point continuum indicating preferences for environmental versus economic priorities (fig. 2). Overall, more than half (55 percent) of the respondents were grouped left of the midpoint, indicating some preference for environmental over economic objectives. Another 25 percent favored a balancing of environmental and economic priorities. These results contrast with research by Shinder et al. (2002a) on the general population in the Pacific Northwest, which found responses more normally distributed along the continuum (i.e., a large majority favoring a balancing of priorities and fewer responses on either end).

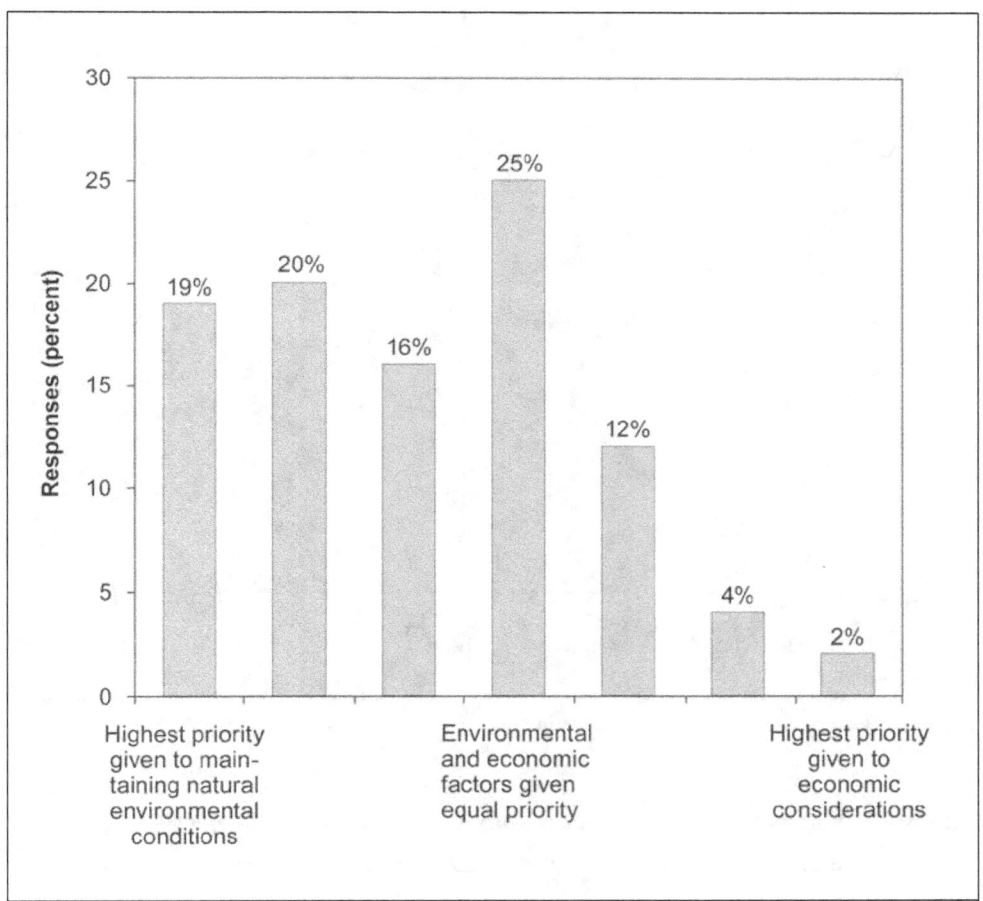

Figure 2—Environmental/economic continuum.

Perceptions of forest health—

Next, we looked at how respondents perceived the condition of federal forest lands in the McKenzie River area. Participants were asked to rank forest condition on a scale from one (very unhealthy) to four (very healthy), or to mark "don't know." Overall, about half of respondents believe federal forests in the McKenzie are healthy (fig. 3). Slightly over one-quarter judged forests to be unhealthy.

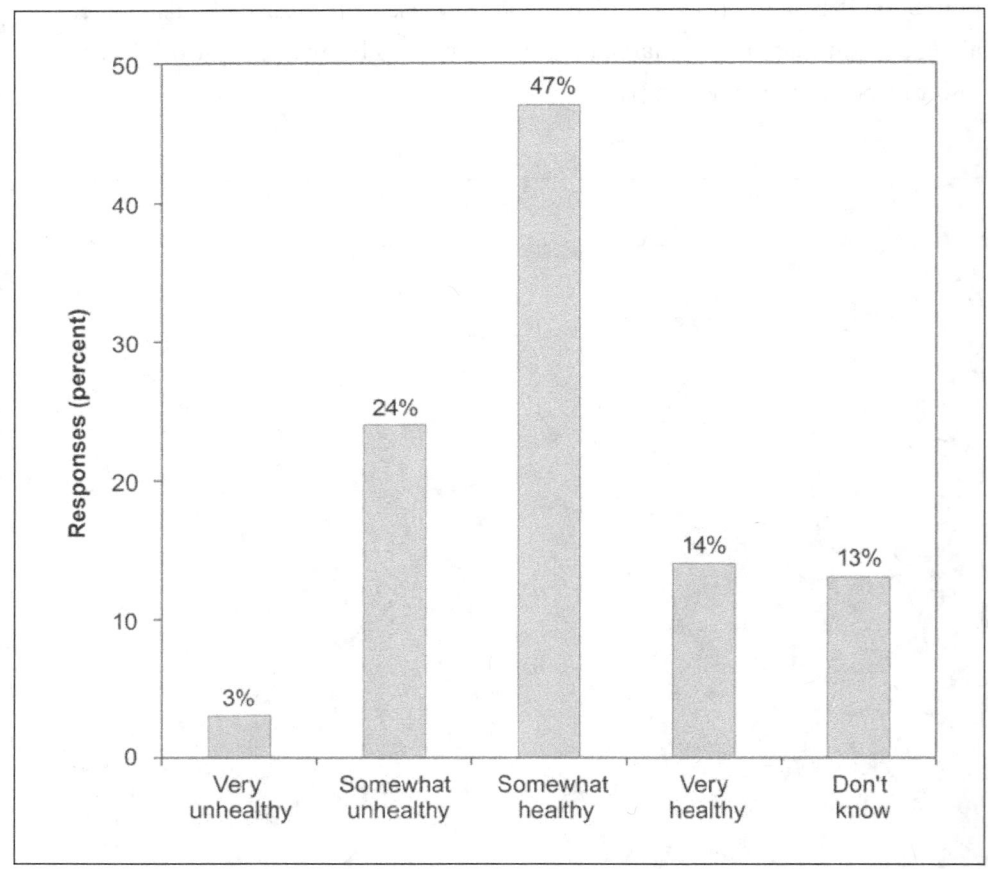

Figure 3—Condition of federal forest lands in the McKenzie watershed.

Knowledge measures—ecosystem management terms and projects—

The purpose of this section of the survey was to assess participants' understanding of the terminology used in forest management and their awareness of existing projects and plans. Respondents were asked whether they knew the meaning of a term, had heard the term but didn't know the meaning, or if they had never heard it (table 2). The first eight terms are general concepts related to ecosystem management, and knowledge levels are high for most. Of these terms, respondents were least familiar with "rotation age" and "uneven-age management."

Table 2—Knowledge of forest ecology terms and projects

	Know term	Heard term, don't know meaning	Never heard term
	Percent		
Ecosystem management terms:			
Watershed	96	2	1
Riparian area	95	3	2
Ecosystem management	91	8	2
Patch clearcut	81	14	5
Forest succession	71	18	11
Active management	71	20	9
Rotation age	66	17	17
Uneven-age management	60	16	25
Disturbance-based management terms:			
Fire-return interval	59	27	14
Adaptive management area	47	33	21
Disturbance-based management	41	31	29
Range of historical variability	40	30	31
Disturbance regime	32	30	38
Management projects/places:			
H.J. Andrews Experimental Forest	64	22	14
Northwest Forest Plan[a]	53	38	9
CCAMA[b]	25	39	36
Blue River Landscape Study	17	40	43

[a] Significantly more Eugene-Springfield respondents indicated familiarity with this term ($p < 0.05$).
[b] Central Cascades Adaptive Management Area.

The second group of terms deals with concepts specific to disturbance-based management. This section was designed to gauge respondents' baseline knowledge of basic terms related to the approach. At this point in the survey, respondents had received no introduction to the concept. Knowledge levels of specific concepts were much lower than for terms in the first section. In most cases, less than half of all respondents understood these concepts, and one-quarter to one-third had never heard of them. Only "fire-return interval" was recognized by the majority, which may reflect the influence of recent education efforts and media attention on the topic of forest fire ecology.

The third section asked about familiarity with management projects or places located in the McKenzie River watershed. A majority of respondents were familiar with H.J. Andrews Experimental Forest, not unexpected given its long history in the watershed and continuing efforts at public outreach and implementation of the Northwest Forest Plan. This plan is the only term with which urban residents displayed a significantly greater level of familiarity than upriver residents. Relatively few knew about the CCAMA or the BRLS. In each case, these levels are lower than those found by Williams in a similar survey from 2001.

Knowledge measures–ecosystem processes—

To further examine participants' knowledge of forest systems, the next section of the survey provided a series of statements about ecosystem processes. Respondents rated them as generally true, generally false, or indicated if they were not sure (table 3). Responses were then scored as correct, incorrect, or not sure. Overall, correct responses to these statements demonstrated high levels of knowledge about the general importance of disturbance processes in forest ecosystems (98 percent) and species survival (80 percent), the value of decadent material in healthy forests (100 percent) and streams (90 percent), and ideal conditions for Douglas-fir (*Pseudotsuga menziesii* (Mirb.) Franco) regeneration (71 percent). In contrast, there were relatively low levels of knowledge (and considerable uncertainty) about historical fire frequency in the McKenzie watershed as well as for a statement where we first brought up the idea of disturbance-based management.

Table 3—Knowledge of forest processes

	Correct	Incorrect	Not sure
	Percent		
Disturbance events (fires, flood, wind) have played a significant role in shaping natural forests in the McKenzie River watershed for thousands of years. (True)[a]	98	1	1
Plant and animal species depend on disturbance events for survival. (True)	80	6	14
Some dead and dying trees are natural components of forest systems. (True)	100	0	0
Large trees and logs in streams are a barrier to fish and should be removed when possible. (False)	90	4	6
Douglas-fir trees regenerate better in open, sunny areas, than shady ones. (True)	71	14	15
Historically, sites in the upper McKenzie River Watershed experienced fire frequently (every 10 to 20 years).[b] (False)	27	35	38
Natural-disturbance-based forest management involves using harvesting techniques and prescribed fire to emulate past events like floods, wildfires, windstorms, and landslides. (True)	53	10	37

[a] Correct answer is in parentheses.

[b] Eugene-Springfield respondents significantly more likely to answer correctly (39 percent) than upriver respondents (28 percent); $X^2 = 6.63$, $p = 0.036$.

Opinions About Management Practices, Citizen-Agency Interactions, and Use of Information Sources

The second section of the questionnaire focused on citizens' opinions about different aspects of federal forest land management, including attitudes about certain forest management practices, opinions about information sources used to communicate with the public about natural resource issues, and experiences interacting with agency personnel.

Factors influencing judgments about management decisions—

Developing a better understanding of how people form judgments about management policies is an essential research question to these and other studies. Thus, we asked participants about factors that influence their ideas about current Forest Service or BLM management actions and decisions. In providing a list of important factors, we drew from the body of research on social acceptability (e.g., Shindler et al. 2002c, Shindler and Neburka 1997, Stankey and Shindler 2006). Respondents were asked to rate each factor as very important, important, slightly important, or not important.

Figure 4 shows percentages for those respondents who rated these items as either important or very important. At least two-thirds believed all of these factors are important influences on their support for management decisions. The highest tier (important to 88 percent or more) included understanding management objectives, environmental consequences of management actions, the role of scientific information in decisionmaking, the place for which an action is planned, and understanding how a decision was made. Overall, these results are generally consistent with earlier findings of Williams (2001) in the McKenzie watershed.

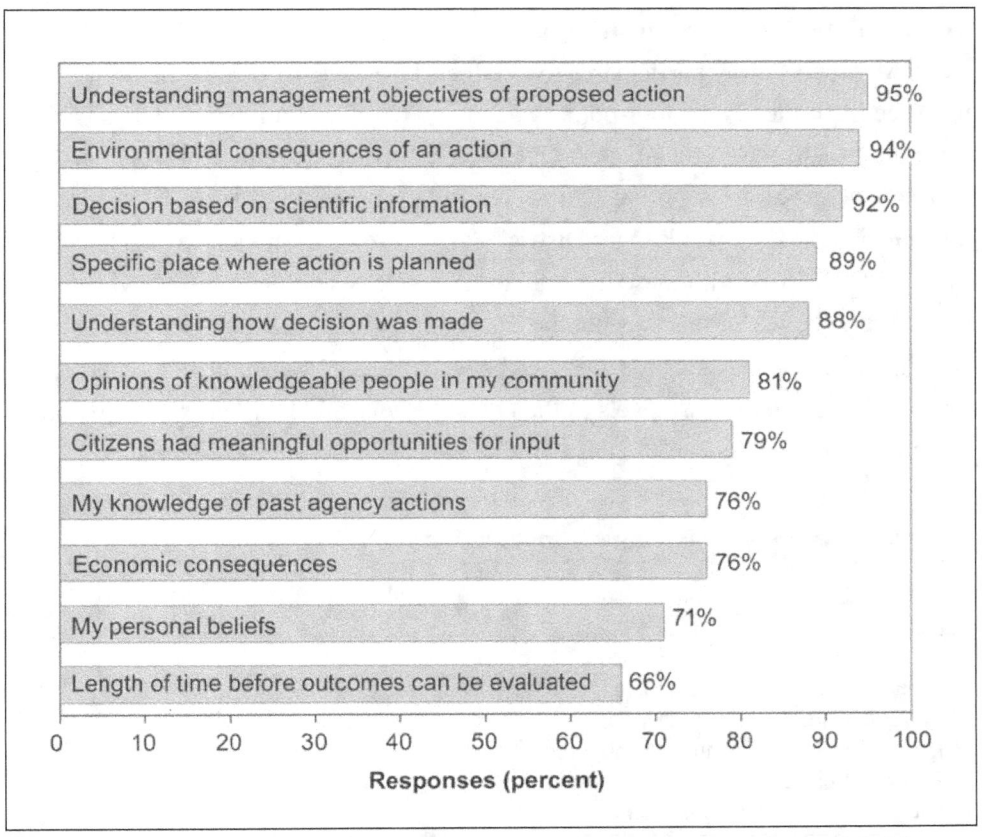

Figure 4—Importance of factors influencing support for forest management actions and decisions (percentages reflect important/very important responses).

Participants were also given the opportunity to list additional factors that influence their ideas in an open-ended format. Of those who chose to respond to this item, many stressed the importance of knowing how politics affected the science used in making forest management decisions. Most viewed political influence negatively, as exemplified by the comments of one respondent, who stated that it was important to know "If an action or decision was heavily influenced by political considerations over objective scientific information…" Another respondent emphasized the need to know that, "…personal agendas and biases…are suppressed in favor of use of sound scientific and economic tools for making forest management decisions."

Responses to this open-ended question were overwhelmingly characterized by a preference for projects that focus on management for multiple objectives over the long term. According to one participant, "I feel it is very important to take the long view, to manage for sustainability over centuries, to preserve species and diversity. I feel that 'old growth' is a vital repository of diversity and it is essential that no more old-growth stands be cut, ever!" Another stated that "Decisions [should be] based on sound ecosystem management, not simply on conifer production."

Trust in natural resource institutions—

Next, we asked survey participants to rate their level of trust in local natural resource institutions on a four-point scale of "no trust" to "full trust" (table 4). Respondents displayed the greatest level of trust in Oregon State University scientists. Over two-thirds similarly indicated full or moderate trust in H.J. Andrews personnel and McKenzie Ranger District staff; however, respondents also had the least familiarity with these institutions. A majority felt the Forest Service was trustworthy; however, this was not the case with the BLM, and this was the only case in which any significant difference between Eugene-Springfield and upriver respondents existed. Trust levels in the Forest Service and BLM are both lower than those found by Williams (2001) in a similar survey of the attentive public.

Table 4—Trust in natural resource institutions

	Full or moderate trust	Limited or no trust	Not sure
	Percent		
Oregon State University scientists	77	15	8
McKenzie Ranger District staff	71	17	12
H.J. Andrews Experimental Forest personnel	67	9	24
U.S. Forest Service	59	37	5
U.S. Bureau of Land Management[a]	46	48	6

[a] Eugene-Springfield residents displayed significantly more trust in the agency.

Information sources—

To obtain further insight into how the attentive public gets and views information about natural resource issues, we next asked participants to rate the level of usefulness of various sources concerning the management of federal forest lands. We explained that "useful" meant sources they pay attention to and that provide good, credible information. First, we asked respondents to rate general information sources (e.g., newspapers, interest groups, university personnel) on a four-point usefulness scale (none, slight, moderate, and high), also providing a place for them to indicate if they had no experience with a particular source. Next, using the same criteria, we asked them to rate information formats often used by federal agencies. For presentation purposes these two groups have been condensed into the same table and arranged in descending order (table 5). The first two columns represent opinions only from those who had experience with a particular source. The percentage of respondents who indicated experience with a source is shown in the far right-hand column.

Table 5—Levels of usefulness of information sources

	Level of usefulness[a]		Respondents with access to source
	High/ moderate	Slight/ none	
	Percent		
University researchers/educators	85	15	93
Watershed councils	81	19	96
Conversations with agency personnel	80	20	87
FS/BLM guided field trips to forest sites	77	23	84
Small, interactive workshops	69	31	79
Environmental impact statements	66	34	86
Newspapers	63	37	99
FS/BLM newsletters	62	38	90
Agency public meetings	60	40	87
Environmental groups	60	40	96
Visitor centers	55	45	93
FS/BLM brochures	49	51	94
Agency Web sites[b]	44	56	77
Timber industry groups	44	56	95
Television	43	57	97
Internet[b]	41	59	84
Radio	39	61	93

Note: FS/BLM = Forest Service/Bureau of Land Management.
[a] Percentages reflect responses from those who had an opinion about a specific information source.
[b] Significantly more Eugene-Springfield respondents found this information source useful.

By sorting the results in this way, an interesting pattern emerges. First, the two most highly rated information sources are university researchers and educators, which corresponds to the high levels of trust in OSU scientists and researchers previously indicated. Second is watershed councils, which is likely the result of the study sample having been partly chosen from the local McKenzie Watershed Council mailing list, but also may reflect the outreach efforts of the local watershed council. Following are three interactive forms of information exchange attributable to agency personnel. Conversations, guided field trips, and small workshops were highly rated here as well as in other recent studies on communication strategies (McCaffrey 2004, Toman et al. 2006). In spite of being a relatively technical source of information compared to other formats, environmental impact statements (EISs) were also highly rated. Although EISs are typically rated low as a useful source (Toman et al. 2006), scores here probably reflect the attentive public's greater attention to these documents and an interest in more specific details.

Two other noteworthy points include the rating of environmental groups as more useful than timber groups and the relatively low scores of visitor centers and brochures compared to previous studies (Toman et al. 2006). This latter item suggests members of the attentive public are apt to seek more specific sources of information on forest projects and plans, rather than the general information given by brochures and interpretive centers. Similar reasoning may be applied to the low ratings received by television and radio.

Overall, these data show that this sample is an attentive group. These respondents use more information sources and formats than participants in a dozen similar surveys throughout the Western United States (Toman et al. 2006).

Forest management preferences—

Public opinion about forest management depends on factors that shape and sustain citizens' judgments about policies and the agencies that will implement them (Shindler et al. 2002c). Thus, we explored participants' preferences for various approaches to forest management. Participants rated their preferences on a four-point scale ranging from "strongly disagree" to "strongly agree," with the option of indicating "no basis for opinion." Responses are displayed in table 6. Interestingly, a majority of respondents (59 percent) agreed that following nature's way is preferable to human intervention in management of forest ecosystems. However, even more respondents indicated that some active management is necessary to maintain healthy forests. Respondents were also largely supportive of forest thinning—only 12 percent disagreed that thinning is a legitimate tool for forest management. Nevertheless, 43 percent of respondents also worry that thinning programs would lead to unnecessary harvesting.

Table 6—Forest management preferences

	Strongly agree/ agree	Disagree/ strongly disagree	No basis for opinion
	Percent		
Following nature's way is preferable to human intervention in ecosystems.	59	34	7
Long-term active management (e.g., timber harvest, tree planting, thinning, habitat restoration, prescribed fire) is necessary to sustain healthy forests.	76	21	4
Thinning forests is a legitimate method for sustaining long-term forest health.	83	12	6
I'm worried that thinning programs will lead to unnecessary harvesting.	43	51	6
Scientific experimentation is appropriate on selected forest lands.	94	2	4
Scientists should take a more active role in forest management decisions.	83	11	6
Timber production is an appropriate use of federal forests in the McKenzie watershed.	67	28	5
Local priorities should have greater influence on management decisions than national priorities.	71	24	5

Almost all respondents agreed scientific experimentation is acceptable on federal forest lands and that scientists should be more involved in making forest management decisions. About two-thirds said that timber production is an appropriate use of federal forests in the McKenzie watershed. Finally, 71 percent indicated that local priorities should take precedence over national priorities for forest management.

Interactions with federal agencies—
Positive interactions with federal land management agencies can contribute greatly to public support for forest management plans and projects. Using a four-point scale ("strongly disagree" to "strongly agree") respondents rated a series of statements about citizen-agency interactions. As before, a "no basis for opinion" option was provided. Results are displayed in table 7 and for presentation purposes are grouped in two thematic areas: (1) communication and (2) openness and relationship building.

Overall, opinions about interactions in both categories were mostly unfavorable. Regarding communication, only about one-third of respondents agreed that agency personnel provide consistent messages on project plans, and 39 percent believe they do a good job of explaining management activities. Forty-three percent believe agency information is up to date or reliable. Nearly half viewed forest management information skeptically because of lack of trust in the agencies. In general, participants felt slightly more optimistic about agency explanation of options and consequences related to forest projects.

Table 7—Interactions with Forest Service and Bureau of Land Management

	Strongly agree/ agree	Disagree/ strongly disagree	No basis for opinion
	Percent		
Communication:			
Agency personnel provide a consistent message on project plans.[a]	32	44	23
Federal forest managers do a good job of explaining their management activities.[a]	39	46	15
The information provided by forest agencies is up to date and reliable.[a]	43	34	23
I look at forest management information skeptically because I do not trust the agencies.	47	42	11
Agency information about forest projects usually provides a good explanation of options and consequences.	51	36	13
Openness and relationship building:			
Forest managers effectively build trust and cooperation with local citizens.[a]	34	49	17
Federal forest managers are open to public input and use it to shape forest management decisions.[a]	43	39	18
I feel the average citizen has no way to influence the agency planning processes.	57	38	5
I trust local Willamette National Forest Service personnel, but I don't trust government at the national level to let them do their job.	64	21	15

[a] Significantly more Eugene-Springfield respondents agreed with this statement.

In the area of openness and relationship building, just 34 percent agreed that forest managers effectively build trust and cooperation with the public, and 43 percent believe agencies are open to public input and use it to shape management decisions. Over half agreed that the average citizen has no way to influence agency plans. The single statement garnering the most agreement (64 percent) reflected trust in local Forest Service personnel but the belief that national-level politics may inhibit their ability to do their job.

Eugene-Springfield respondents reflected significantly more positive attitudes than their upriver counterparts for five of the statements. Note that a sizeable number of respondents chose "no basis for opinion" in all but one category. This suggests there is a substantial segment of the attentive public that is waiting to see how projects play out before making judgments. These cases represent an opportunity for the agencies to initiate a positive interaction.

To further understand these responses, we used an open-ended format to ask participants for suggestions on how forest agencies can improve their interactions with the public. Overwhelmingly, people who responded to this question expressed a desire for more information about forest management projects and more opportunities for public input. For example, one participant stated the need for "…public meetings (small and large) where forest managers listen to the public rather than telling the public what the forest managers plan to do with the public's forests." Several others expressed a favorable opinion of field trips to forest sites, including one who said "I think the guided field trips are very effective and should be done more often!"

Opinions About Disturbance-Based Management

The last section of the survey sought to gauge participants' support for disturbance-based management techniques. This section was prefaced by the following text explaining the objectives of the BRLS and some of the techniques used to emulate natural disturbance.

> We need your opinion about management priorities for the McKenzie River Watershed. To provide some background, the Northwest Forest Plan identified adaptive management areas as places where federal land managers can develop and evaluate new approaches to forest management. The Central Cascades Adaptive Management Area lies in portions of the McKenzie Watershed and contains both the H.J. Andrews Experimental Forest and the Blue River Landscape Study area (BRLS).
>
> The BRLS proposes managing large forest areas (such as an entire watershed) by planning at a landscape level. Under this approach, managers base their plans on natural disturbance events like wildfire, landslides, wind, and floods that have occurred over time. The idea is to use harvesting techniques to create openings of various sizes similar to those created by historical events. One objective is to determine if this approach taken over the long-term will result in fewer risks to plants, animals, water quality and ecological processes than other management practices. On the next two pages, please tell us how you feel about using this type of historic, disturbance-based management approach on federal forests.

The value of disturbance-based management—

To provide a basic measure of the value citizens place on disturbance-based management, respondents used a seven-point scale to rank the value of historical conditions in forest management (fig. 5). On the left end of the scale was the statement "Historical conditions are impossible to reproduce and are of no value in guiding future forest management." On the right end was the statement "Historical conditions are the only ecologically responsible guide for managing federal forest land." The midpoint statement said "Historical conditions are one of many guides that can be used in forest management."

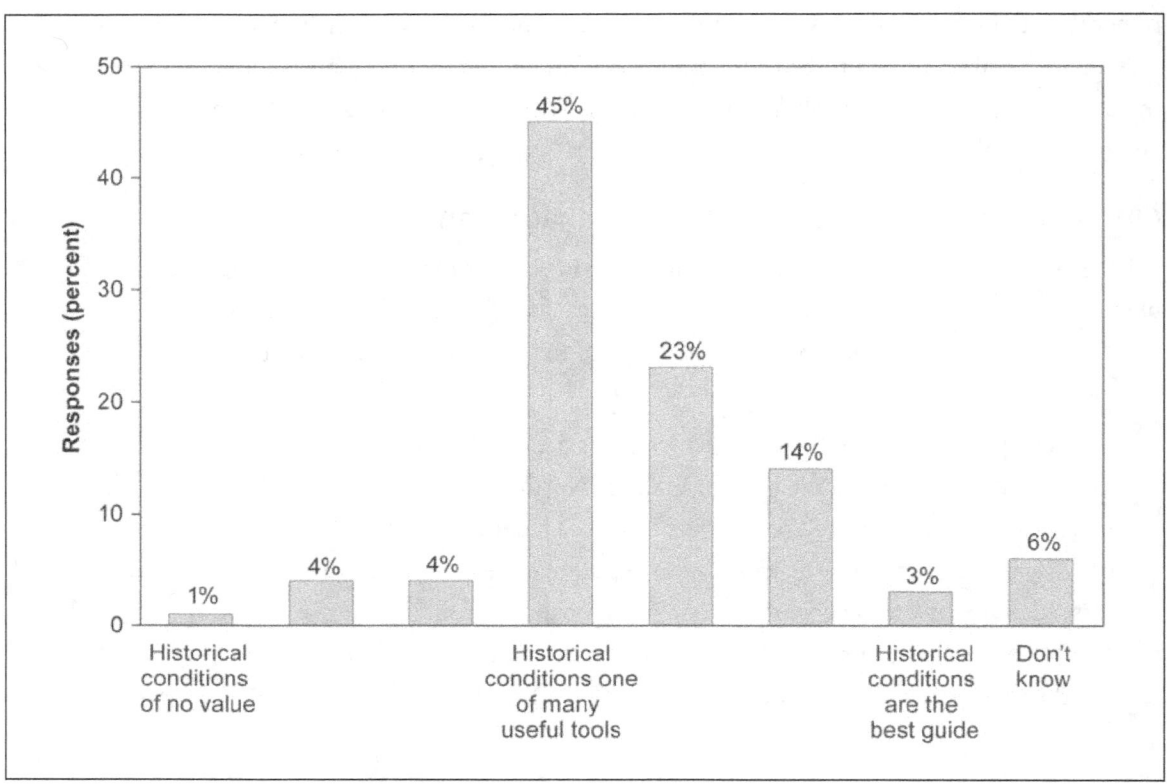

Figure 5—Opinions about the value of historical conditions in forest management. Eugene-Springfield respondents were significantly more in favor of the use of historical disturbance ($p < 0.05$).

Overall, the majority of respondents favored using historical conditions as one of many useful tools in forest management (midpoint of scale). It is noteworthy that 40 percent of the respondents were grouped on the right side of the continuum, compared to just 9 percent who saw little value in this approach. With respect to the urban and rural subgroups, Eugene-Springfield respondents favored the use of historical disturbance in forest management more than their upriver counterparts.

Perceived risks and uncertainties associated with disturbance-based management—

We next asked participants about potential risks or concerns they might associate with the use of disturbance-based management in the McKenzie watershed. These findings are reported in descending order in table 8. Several findings are of interest. The first involves politics and public perceptions. The largest number of respondents (88 percent) expressed concern that national politics would continue to change forest management priorities, and 74 percent felt the public may not understand a disturbance-based approach. Also, trusting the agencies to make good decisions was perceived as a risk by more than two-thirds of respondents.

Table 8—Perceived risks or concerns associated with disturbance-based management

	High/moderate risk or concern	Little/no risk or concern	Not sure
	Percent		
National politics will keep changing the priorities.	88	7	4
The public may not understand this approach.	74	18	7
Potential for harvesting in old-growth stands.	70	25	5
Trusting the agencies to make good decisions.	69	28	3
Agencies will use this new language to justify excessive harvesting.	61	35	4
Too much harvesting overall.	60	32	8
Not enough science in decisions.	56	38	6
Will lead to additional road building in forests.	56	40	5
Not enough public involvement in decisions.	50	44	6
Visual impacts on forests.	45	51	4
The long-term nature of this strategy.	43	44	13
Too many areas being set aside and "locked up" from management.	35	59	6
Too little harvesting overall.	33	60	7
Too much public involvement in decisions.	32	64	5
This approach won't pay for itself.	30	54	16

Additional risks centered on the issue of timber harvest in federal forests and decisionmaking. A substantial majority indicated concern that disturbance-based management might create potential for harvesting in old-growth stands, that it might be used as an excuse to justify more harvesting, that it would result in too much harvesting overall, or lead to more road building in forests. A majority also worried that not enough science would be incorporated into decisions, and that the public would not be adequately involved in decisionmaking processes. Other topics were considered to present much less risk.

Using timber harvest to emulate disturbance—
The final question asked respondents to indicate their level of agreement with a series of statements about using harvesting methods to emulate historical disturbance over large blocks of federal forest land. These findings are shown in table 9. First, the greatest number (85 percent) agreed that forest reserves are still necessary for plant and animal conservation. Three-quarters agreed they would tend to support disturbance-based management plans that were adequately reviewed by scientists and that their support would hinge upon the type of harvesting techniques that were planned.

These items were followed by the specific statement "I support the landscape level historical disturbance approach described above." More than half (58 percent) indicated support. Notably, more than a quarter expressed uncertainty about this question. Meanwhile, slightly more than half expressed confidence that managers have sufficient knowledge of ecosystems to carry out this management approach.

Table 9—Opinions about using harvesting methods to emulate disturbance

	Strongly agree/ agree	Disagree/ strongly disagree	Not sure
	Percent		
Forest reserves (areas with no timber harvest) are still necessary for plant and animal conservation.	85	11	4
I would support this approach if management plans are critically reviewed by scientists.	76	15	9
My support will be based on knowing the type of harvesting techniques planned.	75	16	8
I support the landscape-level historical disturbance approach described above.	58	15	27
I have confidence that agency managers know enough about forest and stream ecosystems to carry out disturbance-based management.	53	33	14
I am concerned that plans based on historical disturbance will be used as an excuse to cut too much timber.	49	45	6
I am concerned about economic losses from timber sales that leave live and dead trees.	31	62	7

Interestingly, 49 percent expressed concern that disturbance-based management would be used as an excuse to harvest timber at excessive levels, somewhat lower than those who rated this as a risk (table 8). Finally, the potential for economic losses generated fewer concerns.

Correlations Between Support and Respondent Characteristics

To further assess influences on public judgments about disturbance-based management, we conducted a bivariate correlation analysis to measure the relationship between citizen support for this approach and the following factors: (1) respondent knowledge of ecosystem project, terms, and processes; (2) trust in agencies; (3) past interactions with agencies; (4) perceptions of federal forest health in the McKenzie; (5) place of residency (Eugene-Springfield or upriver); and (6) education level.

Additive scores were generated to represent support for disturbance-based management as well as each of the knowledge, agency trust, and past interactions variables. For knowledge of projects, terms, and processes, respondents who knew the meaning or answered correctly scored 1, and those who did not know the meaning or had not heard it scored 0. Responses to the other categorical variables (trust and past interactions) were organized on a scale from 1 to 4, where 1 corresponded to negative responses, and 4 to positive responses. Score ranges and bivariate correlation coefficients are shown in table 10.

Only two characteristics, residency and education, had no significant correlation with levels of support for disturbance-based management. Ecosystem knowledge, agency trust, and ratings of past interactions with agency personnel, were all positively correlated with support for disturbance-based management. Therefore, as

Table 10—Bivariate correlations between support and respondent characteristics

Respondent characteristic	Support Range: 7–28
Knowledge (projects)	
Range: 0–4	0.382[a]
Knowledge (terms)	
Range: 0–13	0.346[a]
Knowledge (processes)	
Range: 0–7	0.356[a]
Agency trust	
Range: 5–20	0.389[a]
Past interactions	
Range: 9–36	0.460[a]
Perceptions of forest health	-0.220[a]
Residency	-0.080
Education	0.061

[a] Correlation is significant at p < 0.01.

knowledge of projects, places, and terms increased, so did support for disturbance-based management. Similarly, as opinions about trust and past interactions with agencies become more positive, support for a disturbance-based approach grows. Perceptions of forest health were negatively correlated with support, meaning that respondents who believed federal forests in the McKenzie to be less healthy showed greater support for disturbance-based management.

Summary of Key Findings

The purpose of this study was to examine understanding of and support for disturbance-emulating forest management techniques among an important group of stakeholders—the attentive public. These are the individuals who pay attention to local forest issues and are often the ones who first respond to new plans and practices. Our intent is to contribute to a greater understanding of the factors that influence citizen support for alternative management strategies on federal forest lands in the McKenzie River watershed. To better explore stakeholder characteristics, this study also compared the responses of two subgroups: residents of Eugene-Springfield and upriver communities. Research objectives were to assess (a) stakeholder understanding of natural disturbance processes and disturbance-based management techniques and the agencies that will implement these policies, (b) stakeholder acceptance for disturbance-based management, (c) stakeholder concerns pertaining to the risk and uncertainty inherent in this approach, and (d) potential barriers to future implementation of disturbance-based management. From the findings, we were able to identify a series of important points relevant to these objectives.

Participant Awareness and Orientation

The level of attention local citizens give to forest issues, the priority they place on environmental versus economically motivated management goals, and their perceptions of forest health all provide a context for understanding their ideas about disturbance-based management. Following are some key findings in these areas:

- McKenzie area residents tend to be well educated, and nearly all respondents in our survey pay a moderate to great deal of attention to forest management issues. This suggests we were successful in selecting members of the public considered to be most "attentive" to national forest issues. As such, they are among members of the public with whom resource managers are most likely to interact in formulation and implementation of forest plans.

- McKenzie citizens tend to give priority to environmental objectives over economic ones in forest management projects, suggesting area residents are not motivated to support projects by economic justifications alone.

- Perceptions about overall forest health in the McKenzie Basin were mixed. Measures of "forest health" can be subjective, but in the end, the rationale for using a historical range of variability model will be based on maintaining healthy forest conditions. This context seems to be most appropriate for communicating the historical disturbance message. Indeed, our analysis indicates that as citizens perceive forest health to be in peril, their support for disturbance-based management tends to increase.

Knowledge

The measures of citizen knowledge of ecosystem management in our study are from self-reported scores of respondents. Although this is not an absolute measure, previous research indicates this method to be a fair assessment of citizen understanding of basic issues. Our inquiry into citizen understanding of the terms and concepts specific to disturbance-based management can help provide insight to the context in which the attentive public is likely to assess this approach. Key points are summarized here:

- Although past research has demonstrated that urban residents generally possess greater formal knowledge about natural resource issues (Arcury 1990, Van Liere and Dunlap 1980), our research found few significant differences between Eugene-Springfield and upriver citizens. These results correspond to more recent studies, which suggest that differences between rural and urban environmental values and knowledge are becoming more muted, owing to shifts in rural natural resource dependency and exurban-migration (Brunson et al. 1997, Fortmann and Kusel 1990, Jones et al. 1999, 2003). Increasing numbers of retired residents and commuters to jobs in Eugene-Springfield, and declining dependence on timber income are trends that characterize upper McKenzie communities. Furthermore, education levels over the entire group were quite high, a factor commonly associated with greater environmental knowledge.

- Overall, respondents are knowledgeable about basic forest management terms and concepts. These findings are consistent with individuals who are mostly long-term residents in the McKenzie area, who claim to pay a moderate to great deal of attention to forest issues, and who are well educated. This level of knowledge also may reflect the effectiveness of efforts by Andrews Forest personnel, the forest agencies, and the local watershed council to increase public understanding of stream and river system health. Williams (2001) suggested familiarity with specific terms (e.g., riparian area, woody debris) may also be partially explained by their increasingly common usage among the media and relatively self-explanatory nature. Such knowledge, however, may also be attributed to the attentive public as individuals who consider these to be salient issues and who may exert some effort to become informed. As scientists and managers work to build literacy about and support for disturbance-based management, this heightened awareness may serve as a foundation for understanding more complex ideas associated with innovative approaches.

- Several findings suggest that some of the concepts specific to disturbance-based management are not intuitive for members of the public, even those who pay attention to management activities in the McKenzie. For example, the term historical range of variability (HRV), often used by managers to refer to disturbance-emulating management approaches, does not do much to describe the management technique they intend to use. Citizens may have difficulty visualizing what this approach might look like, adding to their uncertainty about it. This lack of clarity may cause citizens to doubt why disturbance-based management is appropriate or necessary. For this reason, scientists and managers will need to find more direct means to tell the story of disturbance-based management. Indeed, our analysis demonstrates that as knowledge of terms and processes increases, so does support.

- Similarly, citizens' familiarity with specific projects and places in the McKenzie watershed is variable, suggesting that a majority of the attentive public has little awareness of current experimentation with disturbance-based management in the BRLS. It is also likely that few understand the purpose and objectives of the CCAMA, particularly its focus on experimentation. This assumption is supported by low familiarity with the Northwest Forest Plan, which likely translates into lack of understanding about specific land allocations associated with the plan (i.e., reserves, matrix, and AMAs) and the policy context in which experimentation with disturbance-based management takes place. Perhaps more importantly, this lack of exposure to local projects represents a missed opportunity for managers to engage the public in learning about alternative management strategies. Visits to these sites with scientists and managers also can help to establish more trusting relationships and improve communications with the public.

Forest Management Preferences

Many members of the public, particularly the attentive public, possess strongly held ideologies and value judgments regarding the use and management of natural resources (Bellah et al. 1985). Findings of note in this area of our study include:

- It is likely that citizens' preference for following "nature's way" to human intervention in ecosystem processes is related to their values for environmental concern over economic considerations. However, they also recognized that active management and forest thinning are necessary activities for sustaining forest health. Most citizens also believe timber production is appropriate on federal forest lands in the McKenzie, but many worry about the extent to which these activities will be carried out. These findings suggest a cautious support for management actions that involve some level of harvest, even to emulate disturbance. The process by which agencies solicit input from the public in such decisions will likely be a critical factor in building long-term acceptance for any approach that involves timber harvest.

- Support for scientific experimentation and scientist involvement in federal forest management has grown since previous study in the region (Williams 2001). Confidence in the information provided by scientists is also high. This is particularly encouraging for personnel on the CCAMA and BRLS, whose activities are largely focused on scientific experimentation. Indeed, researchers have suggested that demonstrated scientific involvement in management can help create and restore citizens' trust in agencies (Stankey and Shindler 2006).

Citizen-Agency Interactions

Given the perceived level of risk and uncertainty inherent to the disturbance-based management approach, positive public interactions and citizen trust in personnel will be central to overcoming barriers to future management plans. Our findings yielded several important conclusions about citizen-agency interactions in the McKenzie watershed:

- It is clear that trust between the public and agency personnel remains problematic. Of particular importance is that both the Forest Service and the BLM will need to consider their commitment to appropriately engaging citizens in planning activities. This usually involves treating trust-building as a central, long-term goal, not simply as an activity that is pursued on a per-project basis to smooth the way for controversial management objectives.

- Confidence in agencies and the information they provide is also problematic. Nearly half of survey participants agreed with the statement "I look at forest management information skeptically because I do not trust the agencies." Respondents also expressed skepticism about the openness of forest managers, use of public input, and their ability to provide reliable information to the public. This presents an obvious hurdle to scientists and managers working to build support for the use of disturbance-based and other ecosystem management strategies. Research has shown that the public's lack of trust in agencies can lead to increased concerns about the risk associated with management activities (Brunson 1992, Kakoyannis et al. 2001, Stankey et al. 2005) and can undermine efforts to increase knowledge about them. The low rankings overall in this study suggest the need for a more inclusive planning process. Certainly this is reflected in the additional handwritten comments from survey respondents, many of which suggested that agencies should not solicit public input if it is going to be ignored.

- It is important to acknowledge that the McKenzie public's responses about citizen-agency interactions are not universally negative. Many citizens make distinctions between the trustworthiness of local agency employees and agencies as institutions. These dichotomous views of agency credibility are not uncommon (Shindler 2000), nor are they limited to natural resource agencies. Citizen confidence in an institution however, may be shaken by a perception that local priorities will continually be trumped by regional or national ones or frustrations with seemingly impenetrable bureaucracy. Bearing this in mind, our findings suggest that support for alternative management strategies will most effectively be built at the local level, taking advantage of existing relationships between agency employees and citizens while working to build new ones. When discussing the context of project objectives it will be important to emphasize locally based benefits, priorities, and goals, rather than stressing the necessity of projects coming into compliance with regional (i.e., Northwest Forest Plan) or national agency directives. This will also mean listening to local citizens and addressing their concerns.

- It may be relevant that Eugene-Springfield residents held significantly more positive views about their interactions with federal forest agencies than upriver residents. Although past research has found rural residents are likely to have more trust in agencies than their urban counterparts (Steel et al. 1998), our findings concur with more recent studies that suggest this confidence is in decline (Brunson and Evans 2005, Shindler and Toman 2003). For example, Brunson and Evans (2005) suggested that rural residents may be the first to be affected by declines in forest health, such as the incidence of large wildfires and unsuccessful attempts to prevent or control them. These residents may be more likely to perceive inaction on the part of federal agencies as incompetence or an inability to address such problems (Kelly 2005, Shindler and Toman 2003). Other research suggests that frequent transfers of agency personnel or downsizing practices have eroded relationships between rural residents and agency personnel who were once, but now are no longer, long-term members of the communities where they work (Wondolleck 1988).

- Although researchers from the H.J. Andrews Forest were rated particularly trustworthy, nearly one-quarter of respondents were not sure how to rate this group. A substantial segment of respondents also had no basis for opinion about interactions with agency personnel. These figures taken together suggest a lack of contact between citizens, even those who pay attention to forest issues, and important agency personnel in the area. This represents an opportunity for scientists and managers to increase outreach and educational activities at the experimental forest, particularly those related to the BRLS. The advantages for improved communication and trust building are apparent.

Information Sources

Because most agencies have limited time and resources to devote to communicating with the public about forest management, it is important to know which outreach strategies are most effective among citizens.

- The high ratings of conversations with agency personnel, guided field trips to forest sites, and small workshops demonstrate the efficacy of interactive forms of communication. On-the-ground, face-to-face forms of information exchange have met with positive results in numerous local settings, especially for influencing public judgments and behaviors (Shindler et al. 2004; Toman et al. 2004, 2006). Because McKenzie residents believe these activities are useful, agency personnel can move ahead with some assurance that such strategies will help increase citizen understanding and are likely to build support for disturbance-based management.

- Newspapers and newsletters are still relevant forms of information dissemination. However, unlike more interactive exchanges, these mass media forms of communication are more useful for building awareness of programs than for changing citizen behavior (Toman et al. 2006). Numerous written comments on the surveys expressed the desire for more information in these formats. Our attempts to identify a study sample using agency mailing lists indicate a need for improvement in this area as well. We were unable to uncover any comprehensive contact list such as might be used for regular distribution of newsletters or other outreach materials. At present, the Willamette National Forest outreach by mail appears to exist primarily for distribution of Schedules of Proposed Action to a short list of interested parties, many of whom reside outside of the McKenzie River watershed.

- The high ratings of watershed councils and other citizen groups as information sources suggest it may be prudent for agencies to more closely partner with these organizations as a conduit for dissemination of disturbance-based management information. Not only are these groups viewed as useful, credible sources, they also represent access to a network of citizens with which the agencies might not otherwise have regular contact. Agencies may be able to "piggyback" on communications distributed to members of these groups to provide important details about BRLS activities.

Acceptance and Support for Disturbance-Based Management

A primary finding from this study is the cautious support demonstrated for disturbance-based management among the McKenzie River attentive public. There are, however, a number of important qualifications to this support. Additional key findings include:

- Citizens were most concerned about how the influence of national politics will affect the consistency of agency policies toward disturbance-based management. This sentiment was echoed in a number of the written comments on survey forms. This reflects a growing awareness of, and frustration with, the political context in which forest management takes place, where changes in national administration have the potential to substantially alter management objectives and outcomes. Citizens' concerns correspond with the common sentiment expressed by agency scientists and managers in preliminary interviews that it is difficult to manage forests for the long term when political priorities "change every 4 years." Whereas citizens may trust their local ranger district to design plans and projects, they may have little confidence that the federal government will let personnel make good on these decisions (Shindler et al. 2002c).

- Timber harvesting practices associated with disturbance-based management (or any form of forest management) is a primary concern for citizens in the watershed, particularly the potential for excessive thinning, increased road building, and harvesting in old-growth stands. Because some disturbance-based practices in the BRLS were planned to occur in late-successional forest stands, these concerns will be difficult to overcome. Agency participants in our preliminary field tour recognized this as one of the most controversial aspects of the project for some groups in the watershed. Indeed, one member of a local group commented, "Historical disturbance is a very appropriate guide for forest management [and] a valuable tool in forest restoration. My heartburn stems from the way it is being implemented, in old-growth stands and not in second growth where I feel it is most necessary." Although the agencies may debate the accuracy of characterizing stands in certain project areas as "old growth," findings indicate a segment of the public perceives these places as threatened. They are not likely to support disturbance-based management projects on a larger scale without first having these concerns addressed.

- Among the areas of least concern for citizens was the idea that a disturbance-based approach would not pay for itself. This feeling was echoed during conversations on the public field trip to BRLS project sites, where some participants indicated they would hypothetically be willing to see the agency subsidize such projects if the revenue gained from timber extraction were not enough to cover costs. These findings may be important because they suggest that financial concerns are unlikely to represent a barrier to further implementation of disturbance-based management, at least from the local public's viewpoint.

- Currently, most respondents believe forest reserves are still a necessary part of forest planning. Agency personnel must take this seriously—particularly those who believe that disturbance-based management may serve as an alternative to the late-successional reserves outlined by the Northwest Forest Plan. At this point, the informed citizenry has strong feelings that these areas are necessary for plant and animal conservation, and may not support plans that would alter them in a substantial way.

- With respect to citizens' outright support for disturbance-based management, it is too soon to tell. Although more than half say they support the approach, a large segment also indicates they are not sure. These findings have several implications. First, citizens may not have a full understanding of the approach on which to base their judgments. Second, citizens may be waiting to see the outcomes of BRLS experiments before deciding. Third, participants may be hesitant to express support if they feel agencies cannot be trusted. It is clear a substantial segment of the McKenzie public is unwilling to grant agencies carte blanche to implement this strategy without demonstrating their own credibility and the science that justifies disturbance-based management.

Conclusions

Citizens' support for disturbance-based management in the McKenzie watershed will be the product of several factors. Although agency personnel may be tempted to believe that an increase in community understanding of this approach will be adequate to produce citizen support, providing additional information to stakeholders is just one piece of a multifaceted puzzle. Findings here indicate public opinion will also be influenced by the relevancy of planning and implementation of disturbance-based management within the context of local conditions as well as by the quality of agency interactions with citizens (Shindler et al. 2002c).

Results from this study are relevant to local Forest Service and BLM managers because they represent the opinions of residents in the McKenzie watershed communities who pay close attention to federal forest management. However, because the attributes of this group—higher education levels, more knowledge of forest issues, length of residency in the area—may be different from other communities, these results may not be generalized to other agency settings. Nevertheless, as the populations of forest communities throughout the Northwest continue to evolve, influenced by changes such as exurban migration patterns and shifts in local economies, it is likely these findings will ultimately be useful beyond the current study.

The data show that citizens in the McKenzie watershed area may eventually support some form of disturbance-based management. This support is likely to be tied to two factors: (1) the ability of the agencies to provide a sound rationale for its use and (2) the degree to which citizens are genuinely engaged in the discussion. It is apparent the first factor will be better addressed by involving scientists in explanations of these practices, including assessments of potential risks as well as the desired outcomes. Currently the disturbance-based management concept is a nebulous idea for most citizens, and few places exist where the public can see for themselves the short- and long-term consequences of this approach to forest management.

The second factor can be enhanced by the presence of scientists, but the responsibility for improving communications with the public is clearly on agency management personnel at all organizational levels. This task will not be an easy one. Our studies show that over the long term, at least in the last 10 years during which our research team has been conducting social research in the McKenzie watershed, little has been accomplished to improve citizen-agency interactions. Although gains have been made elsewhere in the region by focusing attention on public outreach and partnership arrangements (Shindler and Gordon 2005, Shindler et al. 2004), these typically have been within the context of the threat of wildfire and need for fuel reduction. Conditions are different in the McKenzie watershed, but attentive citizens in these communities perceive little positive change in agency efforts to foster a more open public planning process.

Individual personnel working in the CCAMA are technically competent and well-meaning; however, over the years there appears to have been a shortage of agency commitment to building a meaningful relationship with the McKenzie community. Now, with downsizing and decreased funding affecting all operations, difficult decisions will need to be made about just how much to invest in outreach activities. In any case, for disturbance-based management to succeed, an atmosphere of learning together through face-to-face interaction with communities seems essential (Shindler et al. 2002a). This will necessarily include managers, researchers, and members of the attentive public who represent numerous points of view and will carry the message (positive or negative) to their wider group of constituents.

Within this context, our research identifies several areas where agency personnel may focus their efforts to communicate more effectively with citizens about disturbance-based management.

1. Acknowledge the reality of the McKenzie communities and the important role of citizens who are attentive to forest issues. There is little doubt, and certainly it is no surprise, that public attitudes in the McKenzie watershed lean toward environmentalist values. New management strategies, especially those involving harvesting, will be scrutinized here more so than most other places. Such interest in management activities could be viewed as an opportunity to craft programs that ensure informed public access to decision processes and to further build an ecological literacy among stakeholders (Orr 1992). Most important in this process will be a need to engage the attentive public in meaningful ways. They are already a highly relevant part of the community dynamic, paying attention to agency actions and interpreting what they see for their (general) public constituents. These individuals are the first to respond to any new action, and often do so through sophisticated means. Because they are articulate, this is a group most likely to respond to scientific rationale for alternative management strategies. Seeking out their ideas and experiences will improve the quality of the information factored into decisions (Fischer 2000). These activities also serve as an effective means for building community support and understanding of the disturbance-based approach. Additionally, engaging the attentive public can provide important feedback on public attitudes regarding the eventual implementation of management practices (Molina et al. 1997). As Jasanoff (1990) argued,

> Acknowledging the legitimate role of citizens and their concerns does not diminish the importance of scientific understanding. However, attempts to ignore or discount public judgments of local conditions could undermine consideration of science in political settings, where decisions occur.

2. Clarify objectives of HRV and active disturbance-based management. The HRV concept is not an intuitive one for the public. Under these conditions, it would be easy for agency personnel to simply take the point of view, "Trust us, we know what we are doing." However, the Forest Service and the BLM currently do not have sufficient credibility with citizens to find much success in this approach. There is a need for a more tangible message; for example, citizens will respond better to management actions they can directly attribute to objectives for forest health, wildfire fuels management, habitat protection, and other widely accepted goals. But neither HRV nor disturbance-based management is likely to be the catch phrase that will capture their support.

The current approach may be acceptable on small plots within the Andrews Forest, but to expand this experimentation phase to other settings will require a better public dialogue. There simply are too many questions and concerns about the future of remaining old growth, the potential for excessive harvesting, levels of scientific review, political influence from outside the region, and a general lack of understanding of outcomes.

Such discussion provides room for clarifying the terms and objectives of disturbance-based management. For example, many citizens support "active management" on federal forest lands in the McKenzie watershed. However, it is unlikely that everyone shares an understanding of this idea or buys into how it might play out on the ground. Now is an opportunity to discuss the specifics of a desired approach as well as the existing need for more assertive (active) management in local forests.

This will mean articulating the disturbance-based message in clear and consistent terms. One challenge will be to objectify the concept for citizens by making it specific to their interests. It may be useful to cast the problem with forest health as the central focus and then link this concern to the role alternative management practices can play. Public attitudes and behavior are often tied to the specificity with which policies are presented (Stankey and Shindler 2006). In the abstract, people support good ideas (like biodiversity or species protection), but they tend to really sit up and take notice when these ideas begin to translate to treatments on the ground in familiar places. Five questions that can help clarify for citizens the necessary specifics of planned actions are adapted from Zinn et al. (1998):

1. What local site is involved?
2. What issues drive the action?
3. What actions are proposed?
4. When will it happen?
5. How long before we know the outcomes?

Clear and consistent objectives allow citizens to become comfortable with specific practices and will better prepare them to reach agreement on an appropriate strategy (Shindler and Gordon 2005). Alternatively, failure to clearly convey the motives and details of disturbance-based management for the public is likely to engender distrust, misperceptions of agency intentions, and unwillingness to support management objectives.

3. Take advantage of existing knowledge and concerns to increase understanding of disturbance-based management. The high level of basic knowledge about forests among McKenzie watershed residents is well documented (Shindler et al. 1996, Williams 2001). The current study confirms that knowledge levels remain high, certainly with the area's attentive public. This is also a particularly well-educated group. Findings indicate citizens are poised to receive and understand more specific information about disturbance-based management and the desired ecosystem characteristics of this approach.

The data show that the local attentive public access many sources of information. Overall, they value more interactive approaches, particularly those including key agency personnel, researchers, and local watershed councils. Such interactions on field visits, at demonstration sites, and in small interactive workshops have been shown to be the best methods for changing attitudes and altering citizen behavior toward resource issues such as forest health and fuel reduction activities (Shindler et al. 2002b, Toman et al. 2006). These formats of information exchange are also the most effective for building relationships among parties. This will be important as the attentive groups branch out and carry their informed message throughout their community networks.

An initial tendency among management agencies might be to shy away from outreach activities as they could serve to "stir the pot" of controversy about local practices. Although calling attention to specific projects and practices could mobilize action on the part of certain groups, it should not be seen as creating opposition where it did not exist. Such latent positions are inevitably present and are certain to become overt once project implementation begins (Stankey and Shindler 2006). By being more open and explicit about details during the planning phase, the opportunity is available for discussion, informed debate, and learning. Through these processes, the potential for building acceptance and support exists.

4. Address issues of uncertainty and risk. Uncertainty and risk are primary factors in the public's willingness to accept forest management practices, particularly those that are unfamiliar or untested (Shindler and Beckley 2006). In risk-averse environments, public resistance to programs makes it tempting to overstate the confidence in the outcomes of policies and specific practices. Discussions of the disturbance-based approach will need to be frank about the challenges inherent to this type of management, the consequences associated with it, and the specific nature of the management techniques used to emulate disturbance. Because the ambiguities inherent to innovative types of management can translate into increased perceptions of risk (Kakoyannis et al. 2001), scientists and managers working in the BRLS will need to help citizens distinguish between the uncertainties ("we're just not sure") and the known risks associated with this approach. This will mean that agencies must be forthcoming about difficult decisions and the choices involved.

Citizens' understanding of uncertainty provides a context in which managers and scientists can discuss how mistakes or unintended consequences of experimental management will be dealt with or mitigated. This is best pursued through face-to-face discussion in terms the public can understand. It is important to be direct about the likelihood that something "bad" (e.g., an escaped burn, extensive smoke, altered viewshed) might actually occur and how managers intend to deal with it. If this is done on a demonstration site, it becomes easier to move the discussion to other places where future treatments are desired. People are more likely to accept management activities when they have had a chance to see them in action and become comfortable with the outcomes (Gregory 2002). More open, interactive exchanges among managers, scientists, and citizens will be useful for evaluating potential scenarios prior to policy changes. When given a range of options, citizens can help decide, and will accept, those that work best for local forests (Ehrenhaldt 1994).

5. Focus on improving citizen-agency interactions. People respect and respond to individuals they view as trustworthy. As most everyone recognizes, building trust is a long-term proposition; alternatively, it can be lost in a single action. Thus, achieving a balance point is a continual process of adjustment and working together (Westley 1995). In the case of local forests, the public is looking for genuine leadership from agency personnel (Shindler and Beckley 2006). Citizens want to know that managers share their concerns for resources important to the local community. Agency actions and professional competence are the criteria by which most people will judge the sincerity of these efforts (Stankey and Shindler 2006). In the case of the McKenzie watershed, it is important to remember that trust is effectively built at the personal level. Local personnel can get projects accomplished regardless of how people feel about the larger bureaucracy. A key aspect of this approach is to choose the right leaders for the outreach job and then support them (Shindler and Gordon 2005). The ability to make genuine connections with citizens is a special talent; not everyone is adept at this aspect of the job. Strategies will include creating opportunities to meet the local community in their setting. Be prepared to understand and learn from the public's concerns about issues of local importance.

Perhaps the most important element of building successful citizen-agency interactions will be creating realistic expectations among all parties (Shindler et al. 2002c). This will include redefining the roles that citizens and agency personnel are expected to play in making decisions about federal forest management. McKenzie citizens expect to know more about management than what standard National Environmental Policy Act (NEPA) documents can provide. They are concerned about ecosystem health, but are open to the idea of some level of timber harvest on federal forest lands. They are a complex group with complex perspectives, and many currently believe there are few effective places to share their perspectives about the BRLS and its objectives. Nor do they feel well informed as to what these objectives might be. Meanwhile, the operations surrounding the BRLS have been relatively insulated from citizen perceptions of disturbance-based management under the umbrella of science and experimentation. These circumstances represent an opportunity to employ the flexibility and experimentation of adaptive management and expand the role citizens can play in improving ecosystem health.

It is clear that acceptance of disturbance-based management on the McKenzie watershed is contingent upon whether the public believes it has received credible information about projects and has had access to planning processes. Successfully involving citizens will mean creating a legitimate role for them before management objectives are set in stone and implementation begins. It is also clear that citizens would like to see evidence of scientific involvement and project review. In the end, public acceptance of management practices is not so much determined by the project outcomes as by the processes through which decisions were made (Kakoyannis et al. 2001, Wondolleck 1988). There is no denying this type of citizen participation consumes both time and resources, but there are many reasons to believe these investments will pay off over the long term.

Metric Equivalent

When you know:	Multiply by:	To find:
Acres	0.405	Hectares

Literature Cited

Andrews Experimental Forest LTER. 2002. H.J. Andrews Experimental Forest: Long Term Ecological Research. http://andrewsforest.oregonstate.edu/. (09 December 2008).

Arcury, T.A. 1990. Environmental attitude and environmental knowledge. Human Organization. 49: 300–304.

Babbie, E. 2001. The practice of social research. Belmont, CA: Wadsworth Publishing Company. 498 p.

Bellah, R.; Madison, R.; Sullivan, W. [and others]. 1985. Habits of the heart: individualism and commitment in American life. Berkeley, CA: University of California Press. 376 p.

Brunson, M. 1992. Professional bias, public perspectives, and communication pitfalls for natural resource managers. Rangelands. 14: 292–295.

Brunson, M.; Shindler, B.; Steel, B. 1997. Consensus and dissension among rural and urban publics concerning federal forest management in the Pacific Northwest. In: Steel, B., ed. Public lands management in the West: citizens, interest groups, and values. Westport, CT: Greenwood Press: 83–94.

Brunson, M.W.; Evans, J. 2005. Badly burned? Effects of an escaped prescribed burn on social acceptability of wildland fuels treatments. Journal of Forestry. 103: 134–138.

Cascade Center for Ecosystem Management [CCEM]. 2001. Blue River landscape study: testing an alternative approach. Corvallis, OR: Oregon State University. http://andrewsforest.oregonstate.edu/research/related/ccem/pdf/brlp.pdf. (09 December 2008).

Cissel, J.H.; Swanson, F.J.; Weisberg, P.J. 1999. Landscape management using historical fire regimes: Blue River, Oregon. Ecological Applications. 9: 1217–1231.

Clawson, M. 1975. Forest for whom and for what? Baltimore, MD: Johns Hopkins University Press. 175 p.

Dillman, D.A. 1978. Mail and telephone surveys: the total design method. New York: John Wiley & Sons, Inc. 325 p.

Ehrenhaldt, A. 1994. Let the people decide between spinach and broccoli. In: Governing: a monthly magazine whose primary audience is state and local government officials. Washington, DC: Congressional Quarterly, Inc. 7: 6–7.

Endter-Wada, J.; Blahna, D.; Krannich, R.; Brunson, M. 1998. A framework for understanding social science contributions to ecosystem management. Ecological Applications. 8: 891–904.

Firey, W. 1960. Man, mind and land: a theory of resource use. Glencoe, IL: The Free Press. 256 p.

Fischer, F. 2000. Citizens, experts, and the environment: the politics of local knowledge. Durham, NC: Duke University Press. 352 p.

Forest Ecosystem Management Assessment Team [FEMAT]. 1993. Forest ecosystem management: an ecological, economic, and social assessment. Portland, OR: U.S. Department of Agriculture; U.S. Department of the Interior [and others]. [Irregular pagination].

Fortmann, L.; Kusel, J. 1990. New voices, old beliefs: forest environmentalism among new and long-standing rural residents. Rural Sociology. 55: 214–232.

Gregory, R.S. 2002. Incorporating value trade-offs into community-based environmental risk decisions. Environmental Values. 11: 461–488.

Grumbine, R.E. 1994. What is ecosystem management? Conservation Biology. 8: 27–38.

Jasanoff, S. 1990. The fifth branch: science advisers as policymakers. Cambridge, MA: Harvard University Press. 320 p.

Jones, R.E.; Fly, J.M.; Cordell, H.K. 1999. How green is my valley? Tracking rural and urban environmentalism in the southern Appalachian ecoregion. Rural Sociology. 64: 482–499.

Jones, R.E.; Fly, J.M.; Talley, J.; Cordell, H.K. 2003. Green migration into rural America: the new frontier of environmentalism. Society and Natural Resources. 16: 221–238.

Kakoyannis, C.; Shindler, B.; Stankey, G. 2001. Understanding the social acceptability of natural resource decisionmaking processes by using a knowledge base modeling approach. Gen. Tech. Rep. PNW-GTR-518. Portland, OR: U.S. Department of Agriculture, Forest Service, Pacific Northwest Research Station. 40 p.

Kelly, E.C. 2005. People in the forests: interactions between community and forest health in Wallowa County. Corvallis, OR: Oregon State University. 169 p. M.S. thesis.

Landres, P.B.; Morgan, P.; Swanson, F.J. 1999. Overview of the use of natural variability concepts in managing ecological systems. Ecological Applications. 9: 1179–1188.

Lehman, D.R. 1989. Market research and analysis. Homewood, IL: Richard D. Irwin Publishing. 896 p.

McCaffrey, S.M. 2004. Fighting fire with education: What is the best way to reach out to homeowners? Journal of Forestry. 102: 12–19.

Molina, R.; Vance, N.; Weigand, J. [and others]. 1997. Special forest products: integrating social, economic, and biological considerations into ecosystem management. In: Franklin, J.F.; Kohm, K.A., eds. Creating a forestry for the 21st century. Washington, DC: Island Press: 315–333.

Orr, D.W. 1992. Ecological literacy: education and the transition to a postmodern world. Albany, NY: State University of New York Press. 210 p.

Parsons, R.; Morgan, P.; Landres, P. 1998. Applying the natural variability concept: towards desired future conditions. In: D'Econ, R.G.; Johnson, J.F.; Ferguson, E.A., eds. Ecosystem management of forested landscapes: directions and implementations, Nelson. British Columbia, Canada: 222–237.

Perera, A.H.; Buse, L.J. 2004. Emulating natural disturbance in forest management: an overview. In: Perera, A.H.; Buse, L.J.; Weber, M.G., eds. Emulating natural forest landscape disturbance: concepts and applications. New York: Columbia University Press. 315 p.

Rapp, V. 2003. Dynamic landscape management. Science Update 3. Portland, OR: U.S. Department of Agriculture, Forest Service, Pacific Northwest Research Station. 12 p.

Shindler, B. 2000. Landscape-level management: it's all about context. Journal of Forestry. 98: 10–14.

Shindler, B. 2003. Implementing adaptive management: an evaluation of AMAs in the Pacific Northwest. In: Shindler, B.A.; Beckley, T.M.; Finley, M.C., eds. Two paths towards sustainable forests: public values in Canada and the United States. Corvallis, OR: Oregon State University Press: 210–225.

Shindler, B.; Beckley, T. 2006. Local partnerships for sustainable forestry in Canada and the United States: guidelines for resource professionals. Canadian Embassy Research Report. Corvallis, OR: Oregon State University. 32 p.

Shindler, B.; Cheek, K.A.; Stankey, G.H. 1999. Monitoring and evaluating citizen-agency interactions: a framework developed for adaptive management. Gen. Tech. Rep. PNW-GTR-452. Portland, OR: U.S. Department of Agriculture, Forest Service, Pacific Northwest Research Station. 38 p.

Shindler, B.; Miller, K.; Toman, E.; Olsen, C. 2004. Citizen bus tour of the B&B Complex Fire: survey summary. Research report. Corvallis, OR: Oregon State University. 8 p.

Shindler, B.; Neburka, J. 1995. "It was the most arduous experience of my life:" citizen participation on the Willamette National Forest 1989–1994. Corvallis, OR: Oregon State University, Department of Forest Resources. 32 p.

Shindler, B.; Neburka, J. 1997. Public participation in forest planning: eight attributes of success. Journal of Forestry. 95: 17–19.

Shindler, B.; Steel, B.; List, P. 1996. Public judgments of adaptive management: a response from forest communities. Journal of Forestry. 94: 4–12.

Shindler, B.; Toman, E. 2002. A longitudinal analysis of fuel reduction in the Blue Mountains: public perspectives on the use of prescribed fire and mechanical thinning. Corvallis, OR: Oregon State University. 76 p.

Shindler, B.; Toman, E. 2003. Fuel reduction strategies in forest communities: a longitudinal analysis of public support. Journal of Forestry. 101: 8–14.

Shindler, B.; Williams, R.; Wright, A.S. 2002a. Public knowledge, preferences, and involvement in adaptive ecosystem management. Corvallis, OR: Department of Forest Resources, Oregon State University. 70 p.

Shindler, B.; Wilton, J.; Wright, A. 2002b. A social assessment of ecosystem health: public perspectives on Pacific Northwest forests. Corvallis, OR: Oregon State University. 110 p.

Shindler, B.A.; Brunson, M.; Stankey, G.H. 2002c. Social acceptability of forest conditions and management practices: a problem analysis. Gen. Tech. Rep. PNW-GTR-537. Portland, OR: U.S. Department of Agriculture, Forest Service, Pacific Northwest Research Station. 68 p.

Shindler, B.A.; Gordon, R. 2005. Communication strategies for fire management: creating effective citizen-agency partnerships [DVD program]. Corvallis, OR: Oregon State University.

Stankey, G.H.; Clark, R.N.; Bormann, B.T. 2005. Adaptive management of natural resources: theory, concepts, and management institutions. Gen. Tech. Rep. PNW-GTR-654. Portland, OR: U.S. Department of Agriculture, Forest Service, Pacific Northwest Research Station. 73 p.

Stankey, G.H.; Shindler, B. 1997. Adaptive management areas: achieving the promise, avoiding the peril. Gen. Tech. Rep. PNW-GTR-394. Portland, OR: U.S. Department of Agriculture, Forest Service, Pacific Northwest Research Station. 21 p.

Stankey, G.H.; Shindler, B. 2006. Formation of social acceptability judgments and their implications for management of rare and little-known species. Conservation Biology. 20: 28–37.

Steel, B.; Shindler, B.; Brunson, M. 1998. Social acceptability of ecosystem management in the Pacific Northwest. In: Soden, D.L.; Lamb, B.L.; Tennert, J.R., eds. Ecosystems management: a social science perspective. Dubuque, IA: Kendall/Hunt Publishing Company: 147–160.

Toman, E.; Shindler, B.; Brunson, M. 2006. Fire and fuel management communication strategies: citizen evaluations of agency outreach activities. Society and Natural Resources. 19: 321–336.

Toman, E.; Shindler, B.; Reed, M. 2004. Prescribed fire: the influence of site visits on citizen attitudes. The Journal of Environmental Education. 35: 13–17.

U.S. Census Bureau. 2007. Census data for the State of Oregon. http://www. census.gov/census2007/states/or.html. (09 December 2008).

Van Liere, K.D.; Dunlap, R.E. 1980. The social bases of environmental concern: a review of hypotheses, explanations, and empirical evidence. The Public Opinion Quarterly. 44: 181–197.

Westley, F. 1995. Governing design: the management of social systems in ecosystem management. In: Gunderson, L.H.; Holling, C.S.; Light, S.S., eds. Barriers and bridges to the renewal of ecosystems and institutions. New York: Columbia University Press: 391–427.

Williams, R.L. 2001. Public knowledge, preferences and involvement in adaptive ecosystem management. Corvallis, OR: Oregon State University. 137 p. M.S. thesis.

Wondolleck, J.M. 1988. Public lands conflict and resolution: managing national forest disputes. New York: Plenum Press. 263 p.

Wright, A.S. 2000. Citizen knowledge and opinions about watershed management in the South Santiam Basin in Oregon. Corvallis, OR: Oregon State University. 104 p. M.S. thesis.

Zinn, H.; Manfredo, M.; Vaske, J.; Wittman, K. 1998. Using normative beliefs to determine the acceptability of wildlife management actions. Society and Natural Resources. 11: 649–662.